Praise for *Bagatelles*

"Tom Bonner's poems might appear small on the surface, but all of life is in them. A search for the right button becomes a meditation on mortality. A boy who slams the screen door on his way outside reveals his mother's despair over a future without him.

Bonner is a master at finding beauty and meaning in daily rituals that most of us fail to notice. He is clever and untroubled one moment, mysterious and profound the next. The world he gives us is carefully arranged with color and hard images and people we have never met but still recognize.

Taken individually, these poems celebrate everything from how an egret walks to what a maple leaf has to say. Taken as a whole, they tell the story of a journey from beginning to end.

Bagatelles is a dazzling collection."

—John Ed Bradley,
Author of *It Never Rains in Tiger Stadium*

"The title of this collection suggests that the poems it contains are mere trifles, but if so, this is misplaced modesty on Bonner's part. The shorter poems have the same quiet wisdom of haiku, while the longer ones suggest the contemplative observations of a writer who loves the nature he experiences during his daily rambles along the banks of the Mississippi near his home. These wonderfully wrought verses are anything but 'trifles'."

—Robert Skinner,
Author of *The Righteous Cut*

Bagatelles by Tom Bonner reveals the significance of a thimble filled with brook water and desire. We follow the Emma-Muse into the Mississippi, opened gates, through falling levees. We leave the

Somme into a garden, marble statue, still life of green and black olives, chameleon ready to strike. We might hitchhike on the Jefferson Highway paring our steps into the infinite heavenly numbers with the old school slide rule, Flanders' field, boy soldiers with broomstick rifles, a love's blue blazer, yellow tie, and Hawthorne's rose. Bonner's poems capture such things.

There are love poems. There are subtle yet compelling glimpses of racism, invisible thorns of hate. These are watercolors drawn by the palette of a poet's keen eye, ear, and heart. We sit with Bonner drinking in the Vieux Carré, at ease, as he reads his poems. We find ourselves on a fine thread of language, a canvas of images and human colors. These are playlets of a Third Act. The rare "wild place" pastoral. We hold a "crumpled fedora" and walk, stage left, into a better world.

—Charles Fort,
Author of *Immortelles: Poems*

Bagatelles

Bagatelles

Poems by

Thomas Bonner, Jr.

BOOKLOGIX®
Alpharetta, GA

Copyright © 2023 by Thomas Bonner, Jr.

All rights reserved. No part of this book may be reproduced or transmitted in any form or by any means, electronic or mechanical, including photocopying, recording, or any information storage and retrieval system, without permission in writing from the author.

ISBN: 978-1-6653-0528-0 - Paperback
eISBN: 978-1-6653-0529-7 - ePub

These ISBNs are the property of BookLogix for the express purpose of sales and distribution of this title. The content of this book is the property of the copyright holder only. BookLogix does not hold any ownership of the content of this book and is not liable in any way for the materials contained within. The views and opinions expressed in this book are the property of the Author/Copyright holder, and do not necessarily reflect those of BookLogix.

Library of Congress Control Number: 2022923163

Printed in the United States of America

☉This paper meets the requirements of ANSI/NISO Z39.48-1992 (Permanence of Paper)

Cover photo taken by Author, headshot of Author courtesy of Irving Johnson III, and photo of Author and wife courtesy of Jan Brantley.

1 2 2 1 2 2

Emma Linda Cario, my muse for this collection, read these poems among others in their initial forms as missives from her grandfather nearly every week for more than four years.

Contents

Just a Bagatelle   xi

The Gate	1
Lavender Arms	2
The James	3
From the Somme	4
One Step	5
The Garden	6
Past Our Door	7
A Plate	8
Chameleon	9
Perspective Counts	10
I Dream	11
A Girl	12
Perhaps	13
As He Rose	14
Vieux Carré	15
Another	16
Gathering	17
Not Always	18
Found	19
Her Hand	20
Words Touch Us	21

Aligned	22
To Sligo	23
Vaccination	24
Hinges	25
Departing	26
A Query	27
Poetry	28
Wools	29
Reflection	30
The Rio Grande Moves	31
Rising	32
A Date	33
A Riddle	34
Corporeal	35
Voices	36
Mise en Scène	37
Veritas	38
Socks	39
Emma	40
Her Eyes	41
Numbers	42
Dancing	43
A Rose at Jail's Door	44
Color	45
Paradoxes	46
Ritual	47
Below the Gables	48
Boots	49
Easter	50
Weather of My Heart	51

Silver	52
My Name is Sue Ellen	53
The Trail	54
As She Rose	55
A Hard Village	56
Harmony	57
Ties	58
Still	59
Friend	60
In Her Parlor	61
Her Self	62
Buttons	63
Links	64
Presence	65
Frames	66
A Poppy	67
Afterwards	68
1948	69
From Mabel's	70
Two Soldiers	71
Near Chimayó	72
Wheels	73
Hair	74
From Mexico	75
Moons	76
Acknowledgements	77

Just a Bagatelle

a Gallic nuance

surely a trifle

but more than dessert

brief music in G

by Beethoven or

light lines on a page

even a cottage

facing levees on

the Mississippi

The Gate

On Monday the gate

lifted and water

coursed through the ditches,

the acequias,

invigorating

soil and souls in this

village in the valles.

Lavender Arms

Lavender arms reach

across the brown desk.

Her golden face smiles

as the blue fly slides

down the cool window,

wings still, eyes moving.

Marcy received its

attention, her hand

touching glass like a

flower leaning to sun.

The James

The James flows through my heart

roiling about sharp rocks

careering around snags

seeking the Atlantic.

I watch the water move

as a gray glow rises

like steam rather than smoke.

From the Somme

Mary slipped into her

khaki trench coat

far from the Somme

as stains and rips

appeared on its skirts,

mud falling from the

gun flap on her heart.

One Step

Walking is different

from driving and riding

you feel the grit of Earth,

see trees flowers and grass,

smell cut lawns and supper,

and hear dogs and robins.

One step awakens last week,

a second your next birthday,

a third immortal dreams.

The Garden

I found a word

In the garden

and watered it.

By next Wednesday

two more appeared

making a phrase.

On Sunday more

words joined into

clauses forming

a long sentence.

On Monday I

weeded the garden

and kept a phrase.

Past Our Door

Alice still lives here.

I saw her yesterday,

sinuous black and yellow

lines slipping past our door

as I reached for mail.

Last week she took the sun

as she posed on marble.

A Plate

A green celery stalk

bisects a round white

plate separating

black from green olives.

Chameleon

I watched a chameleon

green astride a long leaf

leap onto a deck chair

and begin turning brown

as her mouth opened then

snapped shut on a black fly.

Perspective Counts

when you're watching

a ball fly through

swinging ship cranes,

the park lying

below levees;

when you hear train

whistles where no

crossings exist,

the broad river

carrying sound;

and when you hold

your lover's hand.

I Dream

across

black nights

in red

yellow

and green

as storm

clouds part

for stars

A Girl

A girl in a pretty dress

A pretty girl

A girl

Perhaps

A him, perhaps a her.

He or she had white wings

above arms of varied hues

and a golden aura

circling a classic head

and smartly sandaled feet.

As He Rose

Ann saw him rolling

up his sleeves as he

rose to answer the

question about race.

The professor thought

he was buying time,

but he was thinking

about the Dred Scotts

and the Black boy and girl

who were not chosen

for the debate team.

Vieux Carré

We walked in wind and rain

while sparrows sought refuge

above and between old

windows and doors and eaves.

Water washed our faces

and drained into our selves.

Another

Why do people wear belts?

Some say to secure what

clothing hangs from the waist.

Others see belts as means

of giving persons shapes.

Still, many imagine belts

as another necklace.

Gathering

Harvest moon above green apples

hanging along gold mountains

while raccoons gather beneath,

waiting for ripe reds to fall,

eyes reflecting lunar light

as they peer through onyx masks.

Not Always

Doug T always ate

buttered grits and bacon

for break

    fast

until he moved to

Portland, Oregon

where cold granola

was served with a view

of the Columbia

River by waiters

who called him Douglas.

Found

Jan sought a room

with a window.

She walked the hall

opening doors

fearing darkness

hoping for light

until she found

the sun warming

her face, casting

her cool shadow.

Her Hand

Her hands held his

blue blazer as

his hands retied

the troublesome

yellow club tie.

She placed the coat

on his shoulders

as her eyes found

her purse across

the dresser near

her cardigan.

His cell phone rang

as her hand reached

to lift her purse,

stopping mid-air,

when his hard voice

left the bedroom

—and her.

Words Touch Us

like burning boughs falling

into a gurgling spring,

steam rising

          vanishing

a branch pitching

toward the sand.

Aligned

The boots I found roadside

stood tall despite worn heels,

their pointed toes aligned

with my starry compass.

First one, then the other.

Soon I stepped through white clouds

as dust fell on old shoes.

To Sligo

His father delivered me:

Peter lay cold and pale

as stone on desert nights.

Among pictures and beads

his crumpled fedora,

like his father's, covered

wide welcoming smiles

of Hibernian men.

A small man under wet

leaves pointed to Sligo.

Vaccination

We wear the mask

to save our lives.

We stand apart

to breathe freely.

We bare our arms

to live our lives.

We act for all.

Hinges

An egret's leg

is unlike mine.

Its appendage

bends back as

foot moves forward.

My knee extends

oppositely

ankle and foot

lagging below.

How hinges know

which way to go.

Departing

The old screen door slams

shaking glasses on shelves

against harmonies of

a coiled ebony spring.

Outside sheets blow in sun,

inside a cake collapses.

A mother with apron

looks through worn wire crosses

as her son disappears.

A Query

Why aren't footballs spheres?

Though they are not round

side to side, end to end,

they move aerodynamically

fitting into armpits

and wrapped fingertips.

But let one hit the turf

--it spins rocks and tumbles,

then still, rests silently,

a ball but not a ball.

Poetry

Poetry is not abstract.

It touches noses and

eyes and ears to

stir our hearts

shake our mental

reeds and invite

us to sit in

another chair.

Wools

The red sweater rested

through summer sun amid

green and blue woven wools

until golden leaves fell

and Robins flew away.

Reflection

The silver key shines in

roadside dirt reflecting

morning sun, capturing

my eyes. As I reach to

grasp it, I wonder what

its metal teeth open--

whether a key fits my lock.

The Rio Grande Moves

through high sands and mesas

heading relentlessly

south among rocks and mud

cutting a wavering line

dividing New Mexico then

making the border to

become El Rio Bravo.

Rising

The roasted browned turkey

rests on a white platter

bordered by pink flowers,

steam rising like prayers,

scent better than incense.

A Date

Sue Ann asked for popcorn,

Jay melted like butter.

They watched *Casablanca*,

leaving only kernels,

and walked along the beach,

as footprints washed away.

A Riddle

I live in darkness

light intermittent

and I grow from roots.

My neighbors and I

are close, living on

matching cul-de-sacs.

We meet often, at

least three times a day,

after which our health

demands our cleaning.

I have sharp edges

unlike my neighbor.

Corporeal

A poet wrote

about her late

love's blue blazer

still having her

corporeal shape.

A college girl

buttoned her blouse

revealing less.

Voices

"Use your outside

voice," she ordered.

My inside voice

rose to rebel

straining between

voiced consonants

and voiceless tones,

glottals getting

in meaning's way.

Mise en Scène

Every class has drama:

the pause before starting,

a professor's first words,

yet this stage includes

first seeing one's students,

an empty pupil's desk,

a question unanswered.

Theater in the round.

Veritas

A maple leaf yellow

or red on limb or grass

tells us the impending

truth about ourselves

who stand beneath the boughs.

Socks

Something about socks

demands an answer:

we know where

they begin but

where should they end?

Emma

Her dog lay on a stair

as she stepped over

him, nearly losing

balance. He lifted his

head to see her leap

below—landing on

the floor by the door

where she struck her pose

to sing her sweet song.

Her Eyes

An orchid graced her arm

while she danced with his hand

pressing into her back.

Though her feet moved lightly,

her eyes never saw him

as her heart carried stones.

Numbers

How do numbers matter?

If you are 19 years

old, what should you do now?

Does 9038

Jefferson Highway tell you

more than my fingerprint?

And does knowing that 12

divided by 4 = 3

resolve last night's bad dream?

Counting to 10 is just

fingers and toes — maybe.

Dancing

Winds blew the sheets away

while clothes pins popped and snapped

dancing on worn green grass

as two pins tightly clamped

a white diaphanous blouse

until one slipped off and

a right sleeve reached for sun.

A Rose at Jail's Door

in Hawthorne's novel

lives beyond its page

as another bush fights

for light in a patio

pot shielded from

sun-warmth, cool rain.

Color

Breeze blowing rouge petals

Butterfly spreading gold wings

Brown eyes showing promise

Paradoxes

The purple bicycle

leaned upon a white fence.

Two green parrots clasped

its handlebar trying

to sing a sad love song

as two mourning doves sat

on the fence trying to laugh.

Ritual

"Are you the one I love best?"

she asked each one gathered

to sing Brigid and Byrne

on their way to marriage.

"No," I and others said

until she came to Byrne,

who taking her hand said, "Yes."

Below the Gables

We walked on West Franklin

searching for bear windows,

round and rectangular,

just below the gables.

Seven years passed until

walking again I saw

a small brown bear waving

at my dog, who looked up

whispering, "That's a bear."

Boots

Her boots rising to her

knees have three magpies with

long, silent blue feathers

entwined among yellow

branches spreading from brown

cowhide stitched tighter than

a taut lariat as

her blue-green, almond eyes

reflect in polished toes.

Easter

I went to Carytown

with four pastel friends for

hot coffee and croissants

to start Easter shopping.

We argued about style,

whether fashion was less,

if spring could be timeless.

Eliot wrote that April

was cruel—what did he mean?

We laughed in Lenten

Sun and sweet aromas.

Weather of My Heart

Stormy weather recalls

an old song and disasters:

winds blowing, seas rising,

trees breaking, home flooding.

The weather of my heart

knows no season, no clock—

neither squalls beyond it

nor dark clouds mar its peace.

Silver

Sliding through black depths

below Lake Oquaba

a rainbow trout followed

silver spinners catching

shafts of sunlight until

seeing a yellow lure.

The trout raced, opening

jaws then snapping them

shut as barbed treble hooks

caught and tightened line

relentlessly tugged up.

Stippled silver soon splashed

as rivulets and

drops exploded before

the landing net restrained

its resolve, its beauty.

My Name is Sue Ellen

but Richard would only

call – me – Sue,

despite my repeating

I would feel warm to hear

him say Sue Ellen in

resonant baritones.

Sue, he said, worked for him,

and I decided he

no longer worked for me.

The Trail

The trail is not mine

nor the river next

to its winding way.

I walk it daily,

my footprints mixing

with others in wet

sand crossed with long vines

like snares of hunters.

As She Rose

Charlotte, finding

her red scarf, wrapped

it 'round her neck,

walked to her horse,

and mounted her.

Soon her scarf flew

as she rose on

stirrups above

saddle and mane,

reins loose, eyes bright.

A Hard Village

In driving to DeLisle

I crossed Bayou Sauvage,

a tale inspiring name,

about a hard village

of Black people (and walls)

struggling to make the sun

shine through darkened windows

thick trees and muddy ponds.

Bois Sauvage, Jesmyn wrote,

a wild place, a wild place.

Harmony

Making music,

Writing lyrics.

A quarter note

lowest on scale

in two-fourths time

and one open

short vowel could

collaborate

in harmonious

composition.

Ties

Janet always wears ties

not secured by clasps

and often flying about.

Reds, greens, or purples flash

across her white blouses

as pale hues escape from

rips in her narrow jeans.

Still

The new drinking fountain

shines from the wall by doors

opening to the stairs.

As I drink clear water,

a Black man waits to drink,

still standing behind

me, still remembering.

Friend

On my resumé I

wrote *friend* but where to place

it—employment, other?

A friend is another

self, a doppelganger.

Although a common noun,

friend needs a proper place.

In Her Parlor

Cecilia's bells

vibrated on

long leather straps

as Lucille's hands

paused above white

keys striking them,

as always, on

her mother's cue.

Her Self

She could not find her hat.

Round and black it would fit

over her long blonde hair

framing her easy smile.

How a hat helps to

present her other self.

Buttons

I remember buttons,

clear jars of discs with holes,

brown white yellow and tan.

My shirt lost a cuff button

and I searched the glass jar

until a pearl-white one

emerged from the clutter.

My fingers could not hold

the button and it slipped back

as my left sleeve flapped,

revealing I was late.

Links

A strand of gray

across the pillow

reminded Rose

of Emily's tale,

a woman past

her time and place.

Rose touched numbers

on her cell phone

but failed to make

her connection.

Presence

The day Professor Braden

wore a black dress with pearls

caused a stir among

her students, one singing

"A-round her neck she

wore a yellow ribbon."

She answered, "Wrong movie."

Frames

Windows and doors,

how they frame us

as we look out,

as we walk in.

Others observe

us in morning

mien when we

depart, locking

the front door like

a camera's shutter.

A Poppy

I wore a poppy

today but not the

real red flower,

and yet the plastic-

covered fabric brought

me to Flanders' fields

where bones mix with earth

and cannon bursts live

in the lines and folds

of other faces.

Afterwards

Wind-blown tree trunks

lay across streets

like dams on the

Colorado River,

holding the flow

until water

lapping at bricks

leached through windows

and rose toward

gutters of homes.

1948

Boy soldiers hiked down

river to Chalmette

with broomstick rifles

and damaged helmets

to defend the city

not from the British

but from enemies

their fathers had fought.

From Mabel's

Through the window

yellow flowers

danced in gentle

mountain breezes.

My desk faced south

and I made notes

about suffering

and redemption

by faithful in

the Morada

hidden by grass.

Two Soldiers

Yousef adjusted his blanket

and looked up the obelisk

where once an old soldier

had stood facing north.

Like the missing statue,

he too had lost a war

not in America but Vietnam.

Huddled against the cement,

He was colder than last year.

Near Chimayó

As gray clouds rolled

over mountains,

a coyote

trotted across

the sand covered

empty plaza.

A dirt devil

swirled rising up

disappearing

while chickens hid.

Wheels

Anna rode her bike

across town to see

her friend Diana.

She thought about wheels

as she looked through spokes:

the silver circles

turning making her go.

Hair

Hair frames faces

blows in the wind

tucks under hats

curls in lockets.

Walt Whitman saw

Earth's green blades

—its follicles—

as more than leaves.

From Mexico

Black bellied

whistling ducks

in shallows

seek minnows

as bright orange

butterflies

on clover

find sugar,

both flying

with love from

Mexico.

Moons

"Moon Over Miami"

an old song touched my heart

like "Moonlight in Vermont."

I remembered many Moons

drawing my eyes like tides,

and once I lost the Moon

but came home to find it.

Acknowledgements

I wish to thank Ralph Adamo, Ashley E. Bonner, Laura V. Bonner, Nicole P. Greene, Katheryn Laborde, Biljana Obradovic, and James Ryer. I owe my wife Judith more than I could ever describe for her affection, support, and expertise — "Thanks, Judith."

Author's Note

Thomas Bonner, Jr.'s most recent book is *Parterre: New and Collected Poetry and Prose.* His poems and fiction have appeared in *War, Literature and the Arts, New Laurel Review, The Cresset,* and other magazines and anthologies. He has books on Kate Chopin, William Faulkner, Edgar Allan Poe, Southern poetry, and Southern fiction. He is Professor Emeritus at Xavier University of Louisiana, where he co-founded and edited *Xavier Review* and its press. He twice served as Distinguished Visiting Professor at the United States Air Force Academy. He and his wife Judith live near the Mississippi River just above New Orleans. They are frequent travelers to New Mexico.

www.ingramcontent.com/pod-product-compliance
Lightning Source LLC
Chambersburg PA
CBHW020545080526
44583CB00013B/1001